UNDER 18
Knowing Your Rights

Michael Kronenwetter

—Issues in Focus—

ENSLOW PUBLISHERS, INC.

Bloy St. and Ramsey Ave.   P.O. Box 38
Box 777   Aldershot
Hillside, N.J. 07205   Hants GU12 6BP
U.S.A.   U.K.

Library of Congress Cataloging-in-Publication Data

Kronenwetter, Michael.
    Under 18 : knowing your rights / Michael Kronenwetter.
       p. cm.— (Issues in focus)
    Includes bibliographical references and index.
    ISBN 0-89490-434-5
    1. Minors—United States—Juvenile literature. I. Title.
II. Title: Under eighteen. III. Series: Issues in focus (Hillside,
N.J.)
KF479.Z9K76 1993   93-6605
346.7301'35   CIP
347.306135   AC

Printed in the United States of America

10 9 8 7 6 5 4 3 2

Illustration Credits:
Aaron B. Cole, p. 61; Brad Conn, p. 64; Courtesy of Senator Orrin Hatch,
p. 85; Library of Congress, pp. 10, 16, 67, 75; Nathan Porath, pp. 31, 33,
36, 49, 72, 81; UPI/Bettmann, p. 12.

Cover Illustration:
Richard Hutchings/PhotoEdit

Contents

Acknowledgements

The author would like to thank the following for their time and their help: Robert Gregg, of the National Committee for Citizens in Education, Washington, D.C.; Devery Quandt, principal of St. Mathew's Middle School, Wausau, Wisconsin; Mark Goodman and Mike Hiestand, of the Student Press Law Center, Washington, D.C.; Cory McClure, of the Youth Law Center, Des Moines, Iowa.

1
Young People Have Rights, Too

The U.S. government was designed to protect the rights of the individual. And yet, for most of American history, the rights of young people were hardly protected at all.

Young people were called minors—not yet legal adults—and they were treated the way that name implies. They were considered less important than adults, and they were granted fewer rights.

It wasn't until 1943 that the U.S. Supreme Court ruled that minors had the same "ordinary constitutional rights" that adults had.[1] But, even after that ruling, courts rarely enforced the rights of young people—particularly when they were in school.

Students' Rights in School

Judges, parents, teachers—and most young people

themselves—assumed that school officials had absolute authority over students. They could control students' behavior, their dress, and even the ideas they expressed.

That situation remained until the 1960s, when it was challenged by a small number of courageous children in Des Moines, Iowa. The 1960s was a turbulent time in America. President Kennedy was assassinated. The battle to end segregation was being fought throughout the American South. And an even bloodier battle was being fought in the sweltering jungles of a distant country called Vietnam.

The military draft was in effect. Young Americans fresh out of high school were being ordered into the army. After a quick period of hard training, they were packed into airplanes and shipped across the world. Within days of landing in Southeast Asia, many found themselves in combat. Before the war was over, more than 150,000 of them would be injured. Tens of thousands would be maimed for life. And more than 58,000 would never return to the United States alive.

The Vietnam war was very controversial here at home. Most Americans supported the war because the government insisted it was necessary. But few people understood the need for it. They didn't see why young Americans had to fight and die in a country almost no American had even heard of a few years before. Opposition to the war was particularly strong among young people. They were the ones who were being drafted and sent to fight half a world away from home. They were the ones whose lives were at stake.

In many places around the country young people protested the war. There were marches on city streets and huge demonstrations on college campuses. Even some elementary and high school students were determined to express their opposition to the war. Among them were several young members of two families from Des Moines, Iowa: John, Mary Beth, Hope, and Paul Tinker, and Christopher Eckhardt. Together with their parents, who also opposed the war, they planned to fast and wear black armbands on December 16, 1965 as a quiet protest against the war.[2]

But the principals of the schools the young people attended got wind of the plan two days in advance. The principals were worried. Many parents would probably be upset by any protest in the public schools. They would consider the protesters unpatriotic, and perhaps the school officials as well, just for allowing them to protest. Other students had brothers, sisters, or friends in Vietnam. They might be angry at the protestors. There would be bad feelings. There might even be fights. The worried principals took a vote, and decided to ban the armbands from their schools.[3]

The Tinkers and Christopher Eckhardt defied the ban. Hope, who was eleven years old, and Paul, who was eight, wore their armbands to their elementary schools. Mary Beth, who was thirteen, wore hers to her junior high, while older brother John, and Christopher Eckhardt wore theirs to their separate high schools. All five protesting students were sent home and told not to return wearing the forbidden pieces of black cloth.

The students were upset and so were their parents. Students had a right to free speech, didn't they? They had a right to express their opinions about the war. The schools had denied them that right. What's more, they had punished them for trying to exercise it.

The Tinker and Eckhardt families went to the Iowa Civil Liberties Union (ICLU) for help. ICLU lawyers filed suit in federal district court. They asked the court to forbid the schools to suspend Mary Beth, John, and Christopher.

The district court ruled against the students. The school had the right to keep order in its classrooms, the court said. Wearing controversial armbands might disrupt that order. "[T]he armbands themselves may not be disruptive," the court's decision argued. But "the reactions and comments from other students as a result of the armbands would be likely to disturb the disciplined atmosphere required for any classroom."[4]

Most Americans, and even most students, probably agreed with the court. The war was not popular, but protest wasn't popular either. Who did these inexperienced students think they were to question the wisdom of the U.S. government?

But the Tinkers and the Eckhardts disagreed with

what most people thought. They believed the young people had a right—maybe even a duty—to question the wisdom of their government. That was what democracy was all about. They appealed the ruling to the U.S. Court of Appeals. That court split down the middle. Four of the eight judges voted in favor of the schools while four voted to support the students.[5] The way the appeal system works, the district court's ruling remained in place. The students could not wear the armbands.

Not satisfied, the two families and the ICLU appealed the case to the Supreme Court of the United States. The Supreme Court has the last word in all constitutional questions. Eventually in February, 1969, the final decision in the case was handed down.

The Supreme Court, too, was divided. Two of the nine justices supported the school officials. Students around the country were already "running loose," complained Justice Hugo Black. Allowing such demonstrations would subject "the public schools to the whims and caprices of their loudest-mouthed, but maybe not their brightest students."[6]

But the other seven justices sided with the students. They had the right to wear armbands. They had the right to express their controversial opinion, even if the school officials didn't like it. "It can hardly be argued," wrote Justice Abe Fortas, "that either students or teachers shed their constitutional rights to freedom of speech or expression at the schoolhouse gate."[7]

The Supreme Court of the United States has the final say when it comes to questions of Constitutional rights.

U.S. Supreme Court Justice Abe Fortas wrote the historic *Tinker* decision establishing that neither students nor teachers "shed their constitutional rights . . . at the schoolhouse gate."

After four years the Tinkers and the Eckhardts had finally won. And they weren't the only winners. The *Tinker* decision didn't just affect the five students in Des Moines. It affected every student in America, and it's still affecting them.

The decision established, once and for all, that the power of teachers and other school officials is not absolute. Young people *do* have rights—even inside "the schoolhouse gate."

But students' rights are not absolute either. In the same landmark *Tinker* decision, Justice Fortas re-emphasized "the need for affirming the comprehensive authority of the State, and of school authorities . . . to prescribe and control conduct in the schools."[8]

So what rights do young people really have? How can they have constitutional rights at the same time that other people have the authority to "control" their conduct? These are not easy questions, and there are no final answers to them. Students, teachers, parents, and the courts have been wrestling with these questions for decades.

In this book we will wrestle with these questions too, presenting the best answers we can. We will examine the differences between the rights of adults and the rights of young people. We will explore the reasons for these

Mary Beth and Paul Tinker, with their mother Lorena, after the U.S. Supreme Court decision upholding their right to wear armbacks protesting the Vietnam War in school. After hearing the news, Paul promptly wore his armband to school again.

differences and consider whether or not there is any need for them.

We will particularly focus on four key rights of major concern to public school students. And we will examine the restrictions schools try to place on these rights. Most important of all we will discuss how the rights of young people can best be established and protected.

2

Understanding Your Rights

There are different kinds of rights.

Some rights are freedoms: the right to do something, or not to do it, as you choose.

Other rights are entitlements: the right to own something, or to try to obtain it.

Who Has Rights?

There are some rights that everybody has. The right to walk down a public sidewalk, for example. The right to practice your religion, or to have no religion at all.

But there are also rights that only some people have. The right to vote, for example, or the right to drive a car.

Where Do Rights Come From?

Most philosophers and religious leaders agree that all

human beings are born with certain rights. The broadest of these are described in the American Declaration of Independence as "the right to Life, Liberty, and the Pursuit of Happiness." These *human rights* don't depend upon any government or law. We are entitled to them simply because we are human beings.

Certain rights, however, are established by laws. These *legal rights* vary from country to country, and even from state to state. In the United States, legal rights are based in the U.S. Constitution. Some of our most important rights are set down there. Others are spelled out in state constitutions or in state and federal laws.

States can make laws that grant greater legal rights than the U.S. Constitution guarantees. But neither the states nor the Congress can make laws that deny the rights granted in the Constitution.

Do Rights Have Limits?

Yes. No right is absolute.

As Americans we have the right to freedom of speech. But the Supreme Court has ruled that we do not have the right to falsely yell "fire!" in a crowded theater. Such speech could cause panic and may result in people being trampled to death trying to escape. The Declaration of Independence demands the right to "liberty," but someone who commits a serious crime can be locked up in prison.

The fundamental legal rights of all Americans—including young Americans—flow from this document, the Constitution of the United States.

Why Do Rights Have Limits?

We all have duties as well as rights. Sometimes our duties conflict with our rights. Parents have a right to raise their children in a religion that does not believe in modern medicine. But they also have a duty to look after their children's health. For this reason, they are not free to deny a child modern medical care needed to save his or her life.

Another reason our rights are limited is the simple fact that other people have rights too. There is an old saying: "your right to swing your fist stops at the end of my nose." The right of one person often conflicts with the right of another. When this happens, difficult decisions have to be made about whose rights should win out.

Do Young People Have the Same Rights as Adults?

Yes and no.

Minors—people below the legal age of adulthood— have many of the same rights everyone else has. They even have some extra rights that adults don't have. For example, they are entitled to receive economic support, either from their parents or from the government. They are entitled to an education. There are special laws to protect them from being exploited (taken advantage of) by employers. Even minors who commit crimes are usually tried in a juvenile court. If convicted, they will probably receive a lighter sentence than an adult would, with the emphasis more on rehabilitation than punishment.

At the same time, many rights that adults have are denied to minors. People under certain ages cannot sign contracts. They can't get married. They can't drink alcohol. They can't decide where they want to live, or who they want to live with.

What's more, parents can do things to their children that no one can do to adults. They can order them around in ways that no one can boss an adult, and inflict a variety of punishments on them if they disobey.

School and police officials also have special authority over young people. In some ways, in fact, school officials have more power over their students than law enforcement officers do. No law enforcement officer, for example, has the right to strike you unless it is absolutely necessary to stop you from committing a crime, or hurting someone. And yet, in many states, teachers and principals have the legal right to spank or paddle students to punish them.[1]

Do All Young People Have the Same Rights?

No. The rights of young people vary depending on their age and the state in which they live.

In general, rights increase and protections decrease as you get older. This is because the law assumes that children become more mature and responsible as they get older.

They become more able to take care of themselves, to control their behavior, and to make reasonable judgments. Therefore, the older they get, the more decisions they are allowed to make themselves, and the more they are held responsible for what they do.

A newborn baby has no control over her own actions, and has to be cared for at all times. No sensible parent would think of punishing her, no matter how annoying her crying might be. As a toddler she will still need to be watched and guided at all times. But she will also have some control over herself. She will begin to deliberately misbehave but her parents will still be quite tolerant of her. The older she gets, however, the less tolerant her parents—and other adults—will be. By the time she becomes a teenager, she will have a lot of independence. But she will also be held much more responsible for her actions. All young people go through this process of gaining ever more maturity, more rights, and more responsibilities as they get older.

There are important landmarks along the way. At age sixteen (in most states), you get the right to drive a car. At age sixteen or seventeen (in most states), you get the right to marry, if you have your parents' consent. At age eighteen (in all states), you get the right to vote and the right to marry even without your parents' consent. At age twenty-one, you get the right to buy alcohol. And at age thirty-five, you can run for President of the United States.

Why Should Parents, Teachers, and Other Adults Have Any Authority Over Young People?

As we have seen, the law assumes that minors are not fully responsible for themselves. This means that other people have to bear much of the responsibility for what minors do. If a ten-year-old girl throws a rock through a neighbor's window, her parents will probably have to pay for the damages. If a high school student injures another student in the hallway at school, the school could be sued for not protecting the victim. Because others are at least partly responsible for what you do, they need to have some control over your actions.

But adults don't just have responsibilities for the children in their care, they also have duties toward them. Parents have a duty to provide for their children and to guide them as they grow. Teachers have a duty to educate students. In order to fulfill these duties, adults need to be able to set some limits on young people's behavior. How could a father protect a toddler from getting hit by a car if he could not hold him back from running into the street? How could a teacher instruct her class if she could not prevent rowdy students from disrupting it?

How Much Authority Do Teachers and Other School Officials Have?

There is no exact answer to this question.

In general, teachers and other school officials have

whatever authority they need to protect and educate children in their care. They have this authority until the young people are mature enough to look after themselves. But the courts say that they must be reasonable in the way they exercise this authority.

"Reasonable" is a word that comes up a lot when courts tell school authorities what they can and cannot do. Teachers can set "reasonable" rules of behavior in class. Principals cannot set "unreasonable" limits on students' freedom of speech. School security officers must have "reasonable" cause to search a student's locker.

But "reasonable" is a tricky word. What seems reasonable to a school official might not seem reasonable to a student. And what seems reasonable to a student might not seem reasonable to a court.

Who Decides What Is "Reasonable"?

It is usually the adult (or adults) in authority who decide what minors can and cannot do. In some cases the adults may be willing to negotiate with the young people involved. But in practice, it is almost always the adult who makes the final decision.

In schools it is the school administration—guided by the policies of the local school board—that sets the rules, regulations, and policies of the school. These authorities may also be influenced by the parents of the students. Student councils and other student organizations may have an effect on specific decisions as well.

School boards and administrators have a lot of leeway in setting policies. But they must act in line with state and federal laws. If a dispute arises, it is up to the courts to decide whether a particular rule or regulation is or isn't reasonable.

How Do You Know What Your Rights Are?

It's not easy.

As we have seen, you have different rights at different stages in your life. Some of your rights are different, depending on where you are and what you're doing. You are free to do things in your home, for example, that you cannot do in public places. In this book we will deal mostly with the rights you have in school. But even these rights will vary from school to school, city to city, and state to state.

There has been a bewildering jumble of court decisions involving students' rights since the *Tinker* case was decided in 1969. Some have expanded these rights. Others have taken rights away. In many situations the law is not clear.

This book will help you understand some of your most important rights. But you may need to consult other sources as well, if you ever feel that your rights are being violated in any way. You may even need help from someone who knows the law in your particular state. Chapter 7 will tell you how to find such legal help.

3

The Right to Privacy

Privacy is the shield that protects us from the prying of other people. It defends us not only from the nosiness of people around us, but from the snooping of schools and other institutions as well. It is often called "the right to be left alone."

Everyone wants the right to privacy. We all have parts of ourselves we want to keep private. We have secrets we want to keep, and thoughts or feelings we only want to share if and when we choose.

The need for privacy is internationally recognized. The Universal Declaration of Human Rights, passed by the U.N. in 1948, proclaims that everyone has "the right to the protection of the law" against "arbitrary interference with his privacy, family, home or correspondence."[1] Here in the United States, the Supreme Court has ruled that a right to privacy is implied in the Constitution, although the word "privacy" isn't actually mentioned in the document. (The writers of the Constitution may have left it out because they took it for granted.)

American courts recognize two different kinds of privacy rights. The first is our right to keep personal information private. The second is our right to make personal decisions for ourselves.[2] But, like all legal rights, these privacy rights are limited.

You have a right to keep some things secret but others have a right to know some things about you, too. The federal government needs to know how much money you earn, for instance, to determine if you owe taxes. Your school has the right to know whether or not you are showing up in class.

Which decisions you have a right to make depends on your level of maturity. A ten-year-old cannot decide for herself that she will leave home. A seventeen-year-old cannot decide for himself that he will get married.

Your legal right to privacy varies, depending on where you are and who attempts to invade it. The courts will protect you from unjustified prying by the government in your own home. But they will rarely interfere with snooping by family members who live there with you.

Before the *Tinker* decision, students had almost no protection from the prying of school officials. Even today, schools chip away at students' privacy in a variety of ways. When it comes to privacy, one educator writes, "an appropriate motto carved on stone above the doors of most schools might be, 'Give up your rights all ye who enter here.' "[3]

Personal Searches

The most direct way schools sometimes violate students' privacy is by unjustly searching them. At any point during your school career, the school officials might conduct a search of your desk or locker. A teacher or other official might demand that you empty your pockets, purse, or bookbag. He or she might even demand that you take off some or all of your clothes!

Take the case of Lisa Rowe, a student at Teaneck High School in Teaneck, New Jersey. One day Lisa found a purse someone had left behind in a classroom. Being conscientious, she turned in the purse to the school office. This simple act of neighborliness resulted in Lisa's embarrassment and humiliation. Instead of being congratulated for her thoughtfulness, she was ordered into the vice principal's office and searched. The vice principal wanted to make sure Lisa hadn't taken anything from the purse. Lisa was even made to take down her slacks.[4]

Only a school official would think they had the authority to order such a thing. If Lisa had found the purse on the street and taken it to the nearest police station, the police wouldn't have dared to search her. The Fourth Amendment to the Constitution protects Americans against "unreasonable searches and seizures" by the police and other public officials. Courts have ruled that police need "probable cause" to search somebody, meaning they need a specific reason to believe that the person is *probably* committing a crime. There was no such reason in Lisa's case. The only thing she had committed was a good deed. The search would have been illegal in a police station.

Even if Lisa *had* taken something from the purse, and the police had found it by searching her, the evidence couldn't have been used to convict her, because of the so-called "exclusionary rule." This rule exists to discourage police from carrying out unjustified searches.

But in Lisa's case the unjustified search wasn't conducted by the police. It was conducted by a school official. Don't school officials have the same limits on their ability to search as the police? Doesn't the Fourth Amendment apply in schools as much as it does in police stations? No, it doesn't.

In a landmark case known as *New Jersey* v. *T.L.O.*, the Supreme Court ruled that the Fourth Amendment *does* apply in school—but *not* in the same way that it applies everywhere else.[5] School officials don't need "probable cause." They only need to show that the search is "reasonable," considering "all the circumstances" involved.[6] They don't even need to suspect the student of committing an actual crime—a suspicion of breaking a school rule can be enough.[7]

Teachers and school administrators, therefore, need much less reason to search you than the police need. What's more, they can consider "all the circumstances." This presumably means they can consider things such as your past record and the way you behave in class. A search that would be considered "unreasonable" for someone else, therefore, might be considered "reasonable" for you.

So, was the search of Lisa Rowe reasonable? Did the vice principal have the legal right to search her, just because she returned a lost purse to the school office? It is impossible to say for sure, but probably not.

Lisa sued, but a trial was never held. Rather than go to court, the embarrassed school board agreed to pay Lisa a sum of money. The money was to make up for the injustice and humiliation she had suffered.[8] No one knows for sure what a judge would have ruled, but the school board apparently believed it would lose in court. The search probably had not been reasonable.

Limits on Personal Searches

School authorities clearly have a legal right to search students. But just as clearly they need a good reason. But what is a good reason? What makes a search reasonable? And just as important, what makes it *un*reasonable?

First, the school officials must have good reason to suspect that a crime has been committed or that a school rule has been violated. Second, they must have reason to believe that this particular student, or students, has violated the rule. And third, the search must not be any more "intrusive" than it has to be in order to find out.

There are lots of things school officials might want to search a student to find. Examples include stolen goods (as in the case of Lisa Rowe), drugs, notes used to cheat on a test, or—more and more often these days—weapons. Looking for any one of these things might be considered a valid reason for a search, depending on circumstances.

Whatever the authorities are looking for, they must have reason to believe that they will find it on the particular student they are searching. Both federal and state courts have ruled out searches in which students are picked at random. They have also ruled against mass searches of all students, or even of all the students in a particular class or grade. On the other hand, having students walk through metal detectors to uncover hidden guns, knives, or other weapons is not considered unreasonable. At least it is not unreasonable in schools where the use of such weapons is a realistic threat.

No matter how good a reason school officials have for searching a student, they still have to do it in an appropriate way. Specifically, the Supreme Court ruled in *T.L.O.,* the method used must not be "excessively intrusive." That is, it must not be more extensive—and embarrassing—than absolutely necessary.

The more serious the suspected offense and the

stronger the suspicion against the student, the more in-trusive the search can be. If a teacher has good reason to suspect a student of stealing another student's ball point pen, it might be reasonable to require her to empty her purse and pockets. It would not be reasonable for several teachers to hold the student down and frisk her.

Strip Searches

Even if a female administrator reasonably suspects a male student of carrying crack cocaine, she cannot ask him to strip in front of her. That would be an offense to gener-ally accepted standards of decency. Strip searches of any kind are hard to justify in a school situation. One judge declared that a strip search of several Indiana students was "not only unlawful but outrageous."[9] Other courts have ruled that school officials, like the police, need "probable cause" to justify strip searching anybody.

Some school districts require school officials to call in the local police to conduct strip searches. This means that they need enough evidence to get a search warrant from a judge.

Other schools have their own security officers. They are a kind of cross between school disciplinary officers and police. This can make things confusing, since school officials and police have to meet different standards to justify a student search. According to the American Civil Liberties Union (ACLU), which standard your school's security officers have to meet depends on their powers. If they have the authority to make arrests, they have to meet the same "probable cause" standard the police do. If not, they only have to meet the "reasonableness" standard of other school officials.[10]

Locker Searches

In general, school officials need less reason to search your locker or desk than they do to search your pockets or purse. For one thing, lockers and desks are physically separate from you. Therefore a search of them is less invasive—less like a personal assault—than a search of your body or even your clothing would be. Several courts have ruled that this means that authorities need less reason to search. What's more, lockers and desks belong to the school. What's inside may belong to the student, but the container does not.

State and federal courts differ on how much privacy—if any—students can expect concerning their lockers and desks. Some courts say that school officials are free to open them up and look inside anytime they want. A few courts have even upheld sweeping searches of lockers throughout the school. Other courts disagree. The Supreme Court has never ruled on this issue.

Because of legal confusion, different school districts have very different policies. You would be wise to find out what the policy is in your community. In the meantime, be aware that what you leave lying in your locker

Many students keep personal things in their lockers, assuming that they are private places. But courts don't always agree.

or desk may be discovered by a school authority at any time.[11]

Drug Testing

In recent years some schools have started using urine or blood tests to check on students suspected of using drugs. At least one New Jersey school district planned to make a urine drug test a standard part of the physical exam all students were required to have. The district backed down after a challenge from the New Jersey Civil Liberties Union.[12]

Like many other issues of students' rights, the question of drug tests has not yet been clearly decided by the Supreme Court. So far, however, courts have usually sided with students who complain that the tests are an unjust invasion of their privacy.

Police in the Schools

As we have already seen, school officials can ask police to come to your school to carry out a search. Except in an emergency, however, police cannot conduct a search on school grounds without a warrant. But police officers don't necessarily have to be invited to come into a school. They can come on their own to investigate a crime, or to arrest a student or school employee.

Questioning

Both school officials and police have the right to question

In recent years, some schools have started using urine or blood tests to check on students suspected of using drugs. So far, however, courts have usually sided with students who complain that the tests are invasions of their privacy.

you about suspected crimes. But you do not have to answer them if you don't want to. If you refuse to answer, however, they may take that as a sign of guilt.

Nonetheless if you are suspected of a crime, most lawyers would advise you not to answer any questions before getting legal advice. And this advice would be the same whether you are innocent or not.

School Records

You leave an enormous trail of information behind you as you trek your way through school. And that information—contained in your school records—reveals more about you than you might think.

If you're like most students, you probably assume that your school records contain your grades, IQ, standard achievement test scores, and attendance record. Such facts are revealing enough. But your records may also contain a variety of other, much more intimate, information about you.

Among the personal data that could be in your files are: (1) a log of any disciplinary actions taken against you; (2) accounts of accusations made against you by teachers or fellow students; (3) reports from counselors who have talked to you about academic, personal, or family problems; (4) health data, including a record of any medical and psychological treatment you've received; and (5) a surprisingly detailed family history.

In addition school records often contain more than

mere facts. Many students' files contain personal judgments such as the following. "Courtney doesn't get along well with other students." "Jim is uncooperative and antisocial." "Andy expresses extreme right wing (or left wing) political views." Some records even contain unfounded speculations about students. "Jan's odd behavior in class suggests possible drug use." "Amy shows signs that may indicate a history of sexual abuse."

Any of this could be extremely embarrassing to you if it fell into the wrong hands. And yet the fact that this information is personal doesn't mean that it is private. Under certain circumstances your school records can be opened up to a wide range of people.

Who Can See Your Records?

Teachers and administrators at your school probably have relatively easy access to your files. In theory only those with a real educational need to see them should be allowed to do so. But, in practice, schools tend to make records available to any school official who asks.

If you transfer to another school your records will follow you there. They may also be sent to any colleges or other post-secondary schools to which you apply. If you try to get a loan to continue your education, the bank or other financial institution may demand to see them, too. Even future employers may want to take a look.

Police, social workers, or other public officials may

Your school records may reveal more about you than you know—and more people may have access to them than you think.

also ask to see your records. In general, schools are not allowed to show them to such outsiders without either a court order or your (or your parents') permission. Even when a court has issued a subpoena, the school is supposed to notify your parents before releasing the information. The only exceptions are when this would be impossible, or in an emergency when someone's health or safety is at stake.[13]

Can You See Your Own Records?

Yes—although you may have to put up a fight to do it. Ironically many schools don't think you should be able to see your own records.

But you don't have to take "no" for an answer. Your right, and the right of your parents, to examine your records is guaranteed by the Buckley Amendment to the Family Educational Rights and Privacy Act of 1974. FERPA, as the act is called, applies to all public schools and to those private schools that receive any federal funding at all.[14] Students in other private schools may not have the same rights, although several states have laws extending FERPA rights to all schools licensed by the state.

If you are eighteen or older, FERPA guarantees you the right to see your own files, no matter where you live. If you are younger, however, your rights are less clear. Some states, including New York and Delaware, have their own laws specifically granting younger students the same rights as those who are eighteen. No matter where you live or how old you are, your parents have the right to see your files—and to show them to you.

This doesn't necessarily mean that you or your parents can walk into the school office and demand to see your records right away. The school has up to forty-five days to give you access to your files. Most school officials, though, will show them to you long before that. If you are not able to get to school to view the records, the school has to mail you a copy. You may have to pay for the copying cost, however.[15]

Exceptions to Rules on Records

Not all school records are treated alike, even under the federal FERPA regulations. For instance, you will probably be forbidden to see the records of examinations or treatment you received from a psychiatrist working with the school. Your parents, however, should be free to examine them.

Neither you nor your parents will be allowed to look at notes made about you by individual teachers or other school officials for their own use, as long as they have not shown them to anybody else.[16] If anybody else can see them, however, so can you.

The right to see school records can be waived (or given up). Families should be particularly careful at the beginning of the year, because some schools send home waivers, asking them to sign away their FERPA rights.

Once such a waiver is signed, the school may use it to refuse to open your records either to you or your parents.

Students sometimes sign away their right to see letters of recommendation written for them by school officials. Some colleges ask students to do this. They feel that teachers will be more honest in their recommendations if they know that the student will not see what is written. But be aware that once you sign such a waiver, you give up your right to see what the teacher wrote about you at any time in the future.

In virtually all other cases, however, either you or your parents have the right to examine any records your school keeps on you.

Correcting the Records

The fact that something is in your school files doesn't mean that it is true. School officials are people, and people make mistakes. They may have confused your name with someone else's. They may have inaccurately recorded a grade or a test score. Other information in your records may be based on unfounded rumors or on the prejudiced opinions of a teacher who doesn't like you.

Still other information may be accurate enough, but irrelevant or outdated. A report that you stole a pencil when you were in third grade is hardly significant even a year or two later. And yet such ancient accusations may stay in your file until you leave the school. Some students have discovered statements in their files that comment on their political or religious beliefs. New Hampshire has a law that forbids schools to keep such information, but other states do not.[17] Your beliefs are no business of the school's, nor of any outsider who may gain access to your files. If those beliefs are unpopular, they may prejudice teachers, college admission officers, or future employers against you.

If you're worried that your school records might contain something damaging or unfair, ask to see them. This may be a good idea anyway, since you never know what mistaken information might be in there.

If you find something "inaccurate" or "misleading"—or anything that violates your "privacy or other rights"—the Buckley Amendment gives you the right to ask that it be removed.[18] If the school doesn't want to do that, it has to give you (or your parents) a chance to present your case before someone not involved in the dispute between you and the school. This hearing officer's decision must be given to you in writing. Even if the decision goes against you, and the information stays in your file, you still have a right to add to your file a letter that explains your version of the matter. Then anytime school officials show the misleading statements to someone, they will have to show your explanation too.[19]

4

Dress and Grooming Codes

Some young people pay very little attention to the way they look. Others spend hours putting on makeup, deciding what clothes to wear, and combing or brushing their hair. But whether or not you're one of those who pays a lot of attention to grooming, your personal appearance can be very important.

Rightly or wrongly many people are going to judge you by the way you look. If you wear ratty, dirty, old clothes, strangers may assume that you are poor and can't afford anything better. If your hair is very long (if you're a boy) or very short (if you're a girl), some people are likely to think that you're rebellious. If your clothes are unusually revealing, some people will make assumptions about your sexual attitudes. And so on.

Your appearance is one of the most personal and

individual things about you. Your clothes and the way you wear your hair help make up the image you present to the world—the way you introduce yourself to other people. They are also reflections of the way you think about yourself.

Whenever you pick a particular set of clothes or decide to wear your hair a particular way, you're saying, "This is how I feel. For right now, at least, this is who I am." You have a right to make that statement.

Your right to control your personal appearance really involves two kinds of rights. The first is your privacy right to make your own decisions. The second is your right to freedom of expression.

School Dress Codes

Virtually every school in the country has some kind of code stating what students can or can't wear and how they should be groomed. Most of these rules are negative, telling you what you *can't* wear. Others are positive, describing what you must wear. Some are very general: "Students shall be neat and clean at all times." Others are very specific: "No facial hair. No cutoffs. No bandannas. No see-through blouses. No skirts with hems more than one inch above the knees."

Some schools forbid clothes displaying logos for adult products such as cigarettes, beer, or other alcoholic beverages. They consider these clothes a form of advertising, and they don't want the school used as a selling ground for products they consider dangerous and unhealthy.

Why Schools Have Dress Codes

Why do schools have these dress codes anyway? Why do they care what the students wear? Critics claim that the main reason for dress codes is to force conformity, to squeeze everyone into the same mold. They argue that schools should be worried about what students know, instead of how they look.

Defenders of dress codes argue that clothing and education are related. They claim that certain kinds of clothes actually interfere with the educational process. Clothes and hairstyles that are too extreme or eccentric can be distracting to other students. This is especially true, they say, of clothes that are revealing, sexually suggestive, or have dirty words printed on them.

At the same time, defenders of dress codes insist dressing well can have the opposite effect. Devery Quandt, the principal of a parochial middle school in Wausau, Wisconsin, claims that students who "dress up a little . . . have a better sense of themselves." They behave a little better, he says. They also work harder. And they're not the only ones; he does too. "I feel more professional with a tie on than I do with a sweater," he explains.[1]

Safety is another reason schools defend the use of codes. They claim that long hair or loose clothing might get caught in machinery during shop class or be ignited by a Bunsen burner in chemistry.

Uniforms

The most extreme of all dress codes is a requirement to wear uniforms. School uniforms are common in many foreign countries. In the United States, however, they used to be confined to private schools. In the past few years, however, some public schools have been experimenting with them as well. So far uniforms have been voluntary in most schools. Most of the schools that require uniforms are below the high school level. But a number of other schools are thinking of requiring all students to wear them in the future.[2]

Defenders of uniforms argue that they cut down on clothing costs for students and encourage school pride. What's more, they reduce the social pressure on individual students who feel embarrassed about how they're dressed. This is particularly helpful, they say, for poor students who can't afford to keep up with the desperate competition for the latest clothes and sneakers that goes on in some schools.

But the biggest reason for public schools to consider requiring uniforms is violence. Certain kinds of jackets, bandannas, caps, or other "colors," are signals that the wearer belongs to a particular gang. Wearing them can be a virtual invitation to a fight. In some city schools these fights have resulted in deaths.

Even clothes that have nothing to do with gang membership can provoke violence. Young people have been attacked, beaten, and even killed for their high-priced sneakers or some other desirable clothing item.

Requiring uniforms may seem like a drastic solution, and it is. But school officials in some troubled schools argue that it is much less drastic than allowing the beatings, stabbings, and shootings to continue. So far no court has ruled on the subject of mandatory uniforms in public schools.

Hair

In some places it's not clothes that are the main issue between the school administration and individual students—it's hair. Young people's hair has been a subject of controversy at least since the 1950s. This was when long hair for boys became a badge of youthful rebellion. By the 1960s hair had become such a powerful symbol that a hit Broadway and movie musical about young people protesting the Vietnam war was actually called *Hair.* In his concert acts Bruce Springsteen sometimes tells how his father cut off Bruce's long hair when he was unconscious after a motorcycle accident. Other young men of the time were threatened with being tossed out of the family home if they refused to cut their hair.

Even today many schools' dress codes try to regulate students' hairstyles. Typically they limit the length of hair for boys, ban dramatic haircuts like spikes and mohawks, and forbid or regulate beards and other facial hair.

Some students resent this attempt to regulate their appearance so strongly that they refuse to cooperate with it. This was the case with seventeen-year-old Brian Wilkinson and his fifteen-year-old brother Travis. The Wilkinsons wore their hair halfway down their backs although the Spring Branch Independent School District near Houston, where they went to school, forbid boys to wear their hair below their shoulders.

The Wilkinsons didn't grow their hair long as a protest. They just liked it that way. In fact they'd had long hair even before they'd moved to Houston in 1987, and it wasn't until the beginning of the 1988–1989 school year that Principal James King, Jr., told them they had to get haircuts. If not, King added, they'd be sent to the Campus Disciplinary Center and forbidden to attend most regular classes and school events.

The Wilkinson brothers thought the hair code was unfair. Why should they either have to cut their hair or be punished? They hadn't done anything wrong. They hadn't hurt anyone or stolen anything or disrupted the school in any way. Besides, they thought, the hair code was sexist because it limited the length of boys' hair, but not girls'.[3]

Their father, Dub, supported them. "I have expected just two things from my sons," he said. "To act responsibly and to use good judgment. I don't hassle them about things like their hairstyles."[4] He tried hard to work something out with King and the other school officials, but they were stubborn. The boys would have to cut their hair or be treated as outcasts.

The Wilkinsons were stubborn too. They were not going to let the school treat the boys that way. If the school refused to let them attend their regular classes, they would refuse to go to school at all. So they set up a learning program at home, and decided to wait out the school authorities.

By this time Brian was eighteen and old enough to quit school. Travis was only sixteen, however, and still legally required to attend classes. The school district filed a criminal complaint against Dub Wilkinson for allowing Travis to skip school. At this point most families probably would have given up, but not the Wilkinsons. Dub stood trial and was convicted. But when he appealed to a higher court, the charges against him were thrown out.

For the Wilkinsons it was a victory—but only a partial one. The school district still had its rule against long hair. The boys still could not return to their regular classes and keep their hair long.

Challenging Dress Codes

The Wilkinson case was an exception. In most conflicts

over dress and grooming codes, one side or the other backs down long before the dispute gets to court.

Students worry that fighting too hard for their rights will result in a bad mark going into their records. Parents, unlike Dub Wilkinson, often side with the school instead of with their children. Faced with a united front against them—at home and at school—the students often decide it isn't worth the hassle.

On the other hand, school officials are often just as reluctant to get into a major battle as the students are. Schools, after all, are in the business of educating people, not deciding matters of fashion. What's more, few school administrations are eager to find themselves in court. For this reason, students who insist on their rights frequently find that the school will give in. In most cases, as Ron and Patricia Olney advise in their book *Up Against the Law*, "within reason, you can probably wear what you want to wear."[5]

There's that word "reason" again. What is "reasonable" dress? A pair of cutoff jeans is one thing; gang colors are another. A boy wearing an earring is one thing; a girl with a two-inch hoop through her nose is another. What's more, some schools—like the one the Wilkinsons attended—have a very different sense of what's reasonable than others have. And they are determined to enforce their code, no matter how much trouble it takes. If you are serious about your right to control your own

Your appearence is one of the most personal and individual things about you. You have a right to choose how you will present yourself to the world.

appearance, you may eventually have to challenge your
school's dress code in court.

What Are Your Chances?

Your chances to win such a challenge depend a lot on
the state—or federal court district—in which you live.
Courts across the country have been about equally divided. In some states, they've tended to rule in favor of
the student. In others, they've tended to rule in favor of
the school.

No court, however, has ever ruled that dress and
grooming codes—as such—are unconstitutional. The
U.S. Seventh District Court of Appeals (in the Midwest)
came the closest to doing this. It declared that "the right
to wear one's hair at any length or in any desired manner
is an ingredient of personal freedom protected by the
U.S. Constitution."[6] Any school that tried to regulate it,
the court ruled, would have to have a very good reason.
The court didn't specify what a good reason might be. A
valid health or safety concern would probably qualify
however.

The Seventh District Court's decision is heartening
for those who believe in students' rights. But it only applies to one portion of the country. Courts in other areas
have ruled that schools have almost unlimited power
over the dress and hairstyles of students. The Fifth Cir-
cuit Court of Appeals (located in Mississippi, Louisiana,
and Texas), for example, has held that hair rules are

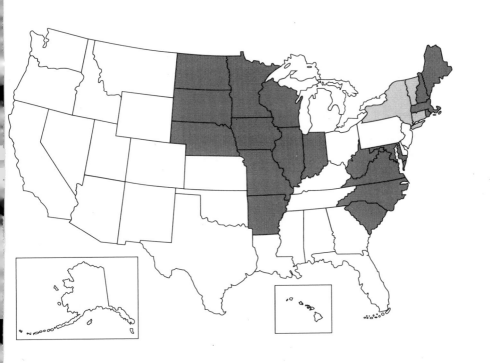

Courts in the dark areas of this map have ruled that students have a constitutional right to choose how they groom themselves. Courts in the white areas tend to uphold school dress and grooming codes. Rulings in the gray shaded areas are unclear.

more or less automatically justified. Among the reasons it gave for supporting the school board was the board's "undeniable interest in . . . compelling uniformity."[7]

Altogether, according to the ACLU, twenty-three states are covered by rulings that strongly support the students' right to decide for themselves what clothes and hairstyles they will wear. Twenty-four are covered by rulings that support the school's authority to decide these things.[8]

Most of the key decisions on both sides have involved hair, rather than clothes. Most often, however, the two issues are treated alike. Where schools have the authority to regulate one, they have the authority to regulate both. Where there is a difference, though, the courts are likely to grant schools more authority over students' clothes than over hairstyles.

There are two reasons for this rationale. A dress code is less drastic because clothes are easily changeable. Limiting a student's right to wear a jacket or jewelry at school doesn't affect his or her right to wear it anywhere else.

Hair, however, is more permanent. Once cut it will take a long time to grow back. A student can't have short hair at school and long hair at home. Hair, as an actual outgrowth of the body, is also more personal. When a school regulates hair length it is interfering with the students in a way it is not when it regulates clothing.

Expressing Yourself Through Your Clothes

So far we've been talking about dress and grooming codes mostly as a privacy issue—the right to make decisions for ourselves. But clothes can involve another right as well: freedom of speech.

People often dress a certain way to make a point or to express a political opinion that is important to them. They might wear a T-shirt with "Save the Whales" or a peace symbol emblazoned on it. They might wear a campaign button with a flattering picture of a favored presidential candidate, or a mocking caricature of a candidate they dislike. Mary Beth Tinker and her fellow students wore black armbands to protest the Vietnam war.

Such expressions don't involve talking, but they are a form of speech. The courts consider them "symbolic speech," which is equally protected by the First Amendment's guarantee of freedom of speech.

Freedom of speech of all kinds—and freedom of political speech most of all—is almost always protected in this country. The First Amendment guarantees us the right to hold any political opinion we want and to express it any way we want. And, in the *Tinker* case, the Supreme Court made clear that this right protects students who express their opinions through the way they dress. Defenders of students' rights, such as the ACLU and the Youth Law Center, say that *Tinker* protects buttons, T-shirts, and other clothes with political messages on them as much as it protects armbands.

But this doesn't mean that anything goes. Courts are very likely to uphold a ban on buttons, T-shirts, or other garments with words or pictures that can be "reasonably" considered obscene (or dirty).

What's more, the rights established in *Tinker* may not always be upheld by lower courts. Despite *Tinker* many judges are still hostile to students who try to exercise their freedom of expression in school—particularly when other students are likely to take offense.

In 1991 some white students at Byrnes High in Duncan, South Carolina, started wearing Confederate flags to school. Some had actual flags hung over their shoulders. Others wore miniature versions of the flags stitched to their clothes. Some African American students objected, seeing the flags as insulting symbols of slavery and white supremacy. Hoping to cool the racial tension, school officials ordered the students not to wear the flags. Over 100 students who wore them anyway were suspended.

The case eventually made its way before Judge G. Ross Anderson, Jr., of the Federal District Court in Greenville. Before the decision was rendered, however, school officials, students, and parents worked out a compromise. The students were allowed to wear the flags to school, but only for three days at the end of the year.

Although Judge Anderson never had to render a decision, he made it clear that he would have ruled against the students. "The schools are for education and not demonstration," he scolded. "We're living in 1991, and if the Confederate flag is a symbol of racism to [black students], then, for goodness sake, put it away."[9]

This case came more than twenty years after the *Tinker* decision. And yet Judge Anderson was apparently ready to deny the Byrnes High students the very right the Supreme Court had guaranteed to the Tinkers and Christopher Eckhardt.

5

Freedom of the Press for Students

Cathy Kuhlmeier and the rest of the *Spectrum* staff knew that the next issue of the school paper would shake up the school. But the students never expected it to spark a controversy that would spread from Hazelwood East High School in East St. Louis, Missouri, all the way across the country and eventually reach the Supreme Court of the United States.

The May 13, 1983, issue of *Spectrum* was slated to contain two hard-hitting articles, each of which explored an emotional subject close to the hearts of many high school students. Several Hazelwood students had bared their souls to the paper's reporters.

The first article examined the lives of unwed teenage mothers. Without naming names it quoted actual students who described their personal reactions to pregnancy and motherhood. "I didn't think it could happen to me," one of the girls had explained. "I can talk to my mother about anything, but I could not face her and tell her I was pregnant." Eventually, however, the baby was born and welcomed into the family. "If I could go back to last year," the student mother concluded, "I would not get pregnant. But I have no regrets. We love our baby more than anything in the world (my boyfriend and I) because we created him!"[1]

"My father was an alcoholic," a student complained in the second story. "My father didn't make any money," said another. "It stinks!" proclaimed a third, expressing the anger and pain they all felt at the destruction of their families.

This was powerful stuff, and the student journalists were eager to see their stories in print. But when the May 13 issue of *Spectrum* came out the stories weren't in it! At the last minute—and without consulting the paper's staff—Principal Robert Reynolds had cut the stories from the paper.

When the students demanded to know why Reynolds had censored their work, he explained that the stories were "inappropriate," "unsuitable," and "too sensitive [for] our immature audience of readers."[2]

Cathy and her fellow journalists disagreed. How could the stories be "inappropriate" for Hazelwood students? The stories dealt with those very students' lives and feelings! The students had described their lives in their own words! There was nothing graphic or vulgar about either article. There was no bad language. And there were no descriptions of sexual activities. What's more, the faculty advisor for *Spectrum* had accepted the articles for publication.

Defying the principal's wishes, Cathy and her friends distributed copies of the articles to the other students. Then three of them—Lee Ann Tippet, Leslie Smart, and Cathy herself—went even further.[3]

Represented by lawyers from the ACLU, they sued the school district. The students charged that the school had violated their constitutional rights. The First Amendment to the Constitution protects the right to freedom of the press, and they claimed that Reynolds had violated this right by censoring their articles.

The case turned into a major legal battle, which eventually became famous among people who cared about young people's rights. The students lost the first round in court. The United States District Court for Eastern Missouri said the paper could be censored by school authorities because it was a journalism class project. But, when the students appealed, the Eighth District Court of Appeals ruled in their favor. The school district then appealed to the Supreme Court of the United States. In 1987 the case, which was known as *Hazelwood School District* v. *Kuhlmeier*—or *Hazelwood* for short—finally made its way to the highest court in the land.

When the Supreme Court makes a decision about a

constitutional right, it affects everyone protected by that right. So it was that the rights of all American student journalists hung on the Supreme Court's decision in *Hazelwood.*

Student journalists and their supporters around the country had reason to feel confident. After all the Supreme Court had a long history of defending freedom of the press. It had even protected indecent and racist writings at times. In one case it had actually upheld a newspaper's right to print top secret documents the government said had been stolen from the Pentagon! Surely the Court would protect the highly responsible stories the students had written for the *Spectrum.*

But it didn't. The Court ruled against Cathy and the other Hazelwood students. And, in doing so, it ruled against student journalists everywhere. Despite the fact that the Court had found nothing wrong with the stories themselves, it decided that the principal had the authority to censor them.

What *Hazelwood* Means

The Court's decision struck a shocking blow to student journalists across the country. It declared, in effect, that student journalists do not have the First Amendment protections that other journalists enjoy. Other journalists cannot be censored, unless they break one of a small number of specific laws against libel and obscenity.

"Libel" and "obscenity" are legal terms with complicated

technical meanings. In general, however, "obscenity" refers to anything so dirty that it is beyond the outer limits of what a community will tolerate. "Libel" refers to an untrue statement that damages someone else's reputation.

What's more, other journalists can only be censored *after* they've printed the material. There cannot be what the law calls "prior restraint"—or censorship—in advance. This rule is important because prior restraint could be used to keep news and information from being revealed to the public.

The *Hazelwood* decision declared that student journalists do not have the same protection against prior restraint. School officials can censor virtually anything that might appear in a school-sponsored publication. What's more, they can do so—as Principal Reynolds did—in advance. All they need is a "valid educational purpose."[4]

This is a very broad permit. A "valid educational purpose" might be almost anything. Among the examples the Court gave of what could be censored was anything that was badly researched, biased, vulgar, "unsuitable for immature audiences," "ungrammatical," or even "poorly written."[5] These examples are so broad that they give school officials justification for censoring almost anything.

What *Hazelwood* Covers

The only bright spot in the *Hazelwood* decision is that it

The tablets that Moses might have brought down from the principal's office.

doesn't apply to all student publications. It only covers school publications that are not operated as open public forums. But what do the terms "school publications" and "public forums" mean?

Judging by court decisions, it seems that almost any publication that is produced with financial help from the school or editorial participation from faculty members can be considered a school publication. So might any publication produced as a class assignment. And so might any publication that bears the school name, or even the school logo.

The idea seems to be that any publication that might be even remotely identified with the school can be considered school-sponsored. If the school is identified with the publication, judges seem to believe, the school has the right to control it. After all, if readers are offended by what appears in the publication, they might blame the school. The only way the school can protect itself is by exercising control.

But even a school publication should be free of school censorship if it is also a "public forum." That is if—by "policy or practice"—it allows all students to express any opinion on any topic.[6] If it is a true public forum then no one—school official or not—has the right to censor it.

Judges, however, have been very reluctant to recognize school publications as public forums. They have used almost any excuse not to do so. If you want your school publication to be accepted as one, you need to make very clear—in advance—that it is open to the expression of any opinion, not just those that the editors or school officials agree with. The key words to use are "open," "public," and "unrestricted."

If possible, convince school officials to describe the publication as a "public forum" in some document. It might be difficult to get their cooperation, however, since they are the ones most likely to want to censor the publication later.

Steps like those just mentioned can establish a public forum "by policy." But the publication must also be a public forum "by practice." This means it has to actually publish controversial opinions, including those the editors, faculty advisors, and other officials disagree with.

None of this means, however, that the editors can't make normal editorial judgments about what goes in the publication. They can still edit the contents for style, grammar, length, quality of writing, and so on. But they can't, in any way, censor contents because they object to *what* is being said or *who* is saying it.

Once a public forum is established, students expressing themselves there should be fully protected by the First Amendment.

Going Underground

What if your publication is not in any way connected to the school? What if it is a totally underground publication,

Administrators' censorship of the contents of school newspapers is a problem for student journalism across the country.

written in your home, by you and some fellow journalists, and run off on a copy machine at your mom's office? This kind of publication is called underground.

If yours is an underground publication, you are free to publish anything you want in it. Anything, that is, that could be legally published by an adult. As we have seen, no one is free to publish anything that is obscene or libelous. There is also a real question about whether students are free to publish anything that encourages other students to commit a crime or to break a legal school rule.

Aside from these restrictions, however, your underground paper should be fully protected by the First Amendment. You may run into trouble, however, if you attempt to distribute an underground publication on school property or at a school-sponsored event. School officials often argue that distributing controversial underground publications can result in disruption of school activities.

For this reason, some schools require students who want to distribute underground material to submit it for approval in advance. But in a case involving an underground paper called *Bad Astra*,[7] a federal court forbid this kind of prior restraint of a non-school publication. The court, however, made clear that schools could still regulate *when* and *where* students could distribute such material on school grounds. They just couldn't approve (or censor) the contents. What's more, if the material does result in disruption, the schools have the authority to punish the students afterward.[8]

The Risks You Run

Journalism can be a risky business. Throughout American history, journalists have been subjected to threats, scorn, and punishment for daring to exercise freedom of the press. As far back as 1734 John Peter Zenger was thrown into prison for publishing criticism of the governor of the New York colony. A century later the anti-slavery editor, Elijah Lovejoy, was murdered by a pro-slavery mob in Alton, Illinois. In this century hundreds of journalists have been sued, beaten, murdered, or jailed in the practice of their craft.

What risks do you face, as a student journalist, if you publish something disapproved of by school officials? Fortunately you're not likely to be beaten or thrown into jail. But you do run the risk that the school administration will take action against you or your publication, or both.

The most likely thing to happen is that your work will be censored. If your material is submitted to school officials in advance, as the *Spectrum* was, it may never see print. If it is not, copies of the controversial publication may be confiscated as soon as they appear.

These things are bad enough, but you could also find yourself personally disciplined for defying your school administration. Students have been dismissed from their

Journalism can be a risky business. As far back as 1734, John Peter
Zenger was tried and thrown into prison for publishing criticism of
the governor of New York Colony.

A century later, the anti-slavery editor, Elijah Lovejoy, was
murdered by a pro-slavery mob in Alton, Illinois.

positions on the staffs of school publications; underground journalists have been suspended for attempting to distribute their work on school property.

Matthew Roberts was put on "suspended expulsion" for helping to write and distribute an underground journal called *Wacked* on the campus of Beverly Hills High School in 1992. The school board apparently found the five-page paper vulgar and racially intolerant.[9]

Jennifer Wertz and four other students were suspended from the Hollidaysburg Area High School in Pennsylvania for distributing their own underground paper, *Tell All.* The principal, Gary Robinson, denied that the suspension had anything to do with the fact that he and his school administration had been criticized in the paper. Instead, he said, it was because the students had not submitted the paper for approval before they distributed it on campus.[10] And this was done despite the ruling on the *Bad Astra* case years before.

According to Mark Goodman, of the Student Press Law Center, most cases of student journalists being suspended or expelled involve underground publications like these.[11] That's because schools usually have some kind of review policy in place that keeps things the administration objects to from appearing in school publications in the first place. But the fact that you're working for a school publication doesn't necessarily mean you're safe.

Take the case of Colin Murphy. In 1983 Colin was a

junior at Cumberland High School in Cumberland, Rhode Island, and the editor of the school paper, *The Clipper Courier*. He published an article that criticized a school committeeman named William J. O'Coin for skipping several committee meetings. O'Coin, who denied the charges, sued Colin for $200,000 in damages![12] The case was eventually settled out of court, and Colin never had to pay any money.[13] But the suit was a chilling reminder of the risks that student journalists can run.

State by State

Protections for student journalists vary drastically from state to state. In the wake of the *Hazelwood* case, Colorado, Iowa, Massachusetts, and Kansas quickly passed laws giving students some of the press freedoms *Hazelwood* took away. California already had such a law. Wisconsin and New Jersey seem close to passing laws of their own, and there are strong movements pushing for similar laws in several other states.[14]

Elsewhere, however, things are going in the opposite direction. Student free press bills have been killed in some states, and two high school journalism advisers recently lost an important case in a federal court in Michigan. "I don't think there are students' rights anymore," their discouraged lawyer complained. "[T]he pendulum is just swinging absolutely the other way."[15]

6

Your Rights in the Classroom

You and your teachers each have your own rights and duties in the classroom. Your most important right—and duty—is to learn. Your teacher's most important duty is to teach.

What goes on in the classroom is designed to allow the teaching and learning processes to take place. This is why courts have given teachers lots of leeway to decide what should go on in the classroom, and how to set rules of behavior for their students. As long as these rules are reasonable, you have to obey them. This is what Justice Fortas meant when he wrote that school officials had the right "to prescribe and control conduct in the schools."[1]

Your Duties in Class

Along with the right to learn comes the obligation to try

to learn. Your first duty in the classroom is to be there. You are legally required to be present in your assigned classes, except when properly excused. For most people this legal obligation lasts until they reach a particular age, set by their state, or graduate from high school—whichever comes first.

There are some exceptions. Parents can receive permission to teach their children at home. Severe physical or mental problems can make it impossible for a child to attend an ordinary school. Formal vocational training can sometimes substitute for all or part of your high school obligation. But, for most students, there is no legal way out of the obligation to attend school.

While you are in school you have to do your homework and other reasonable work assigned to you.[2] If you don't, your teacher is free to lower your grade accordingly. If you fail to do enough of the assigned work, you can be flunked.

You're not the only one with the right to learn. Every other student has the same right. This is why you have a responsibility not to interfere with your fellow students' opportunity to learn. This means that you mustn't do anything that might disrupt the class or distract others from listening to the teacher, studying, doing classwork, or performing other school-related activities. They, in turn, have the duty not to disrupt or distract you.

This right to be free of distraction sometimes has to

Every student has the right to learn. This means that, in most circumstances, students must refrain from disrupting the class or distracting others from the teaching and learning process.

be balanced against other rights. This was true in the *Tinker* case, for example. The fact that Mary Beth Tinker and the others wore controversial armbands might very well have distracted other students. It may even have angered them. But, the Supreme Court decided, their right not to be distracted had to bow to the protestors' right to express opposition to the Vietnam war.

The Court probably would have ruled differently if the protesting students had done something more disruptive to express their opinion. If they'd tried to block other students from going to class, for example, or interrupted a school assembly by singing an anti-war song. As always when rights are in conflict, it was a matter of balance.

Your Right to "Due Process"

You are required to obey the legal rules and directions of your teachers. If you break them, they have the right to discipline you. But teachers and other school officials have to follow rules too.

The Fourteenth Amendment of the Constitution gives everyone the right to "due process" under the law. This means that government institutions cannot punish or penalize you, except according to just rules and procedures. Public schools are government institutions, and so they must give students "due process" too.

In practice this means that school rules and punishments

must be reasonable, and that you must be given a chance to defend yourself from unjust charges.

Before they can legally punish you, school officials should be able to demonstrate two things. First, that you violated some specific rule or policy. And second, that the punishment is appropriate for that offense.

Just what procedures officials need to follow in each case depends on the circumstances. A minor punishment requires very little "due process." A teacher's word is usually enough to justify keeping you after school for talking in class. On the other hand, you would be entitled to an extensive hearing before the school could suspend you for a long time or expel you altogether. You have a right to go to school, and it cannot be taken away from you without a very good reason.

Before punishing you, school officials must tell you what they think you did wrong and why they think so. In most cases you should have a chance to respond to the charge before the punishment begins. There are two major exceptions to this, however. One is in the case of repeated misbehavior. Another is when a threat to anyone's health or safety is involved. If you are doing something that is endangering yourself or anyone else, the authorities have the right to stop you immediately. The usual rules of due process don't necessarily apply. Eventually, however, you will still have to be given a chance to defend yourself.

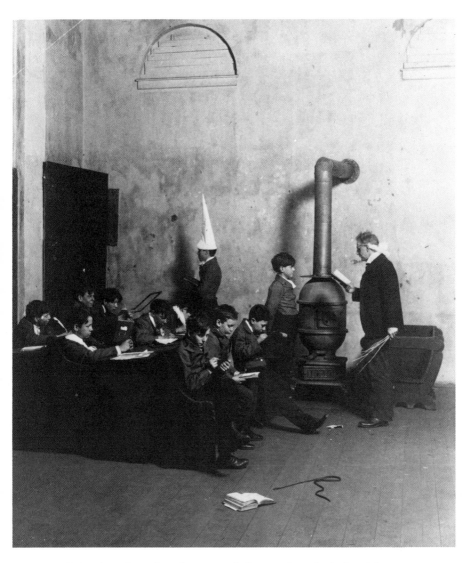

It used to be taken for granted that teachers had the right to humiliate, and even to whip their students.

Questioning Your Punishment

School authorities clearly have the right to discipline you, but that discipline must be reasonable. When you break a rule, you should expect to pay a penalty, but you should not accept unjust charges and unfair penalties. How can you defend yourself against them? For that matter, how can you tell whether a particular charge or punishment is reasonable or not?

There are several questions to ask. The most obvious question is: Are you guilty? In other words did you do what you are accused of doing? Innocence is an absolute defense.

But there are other questions as well. First, did what you are accused of doing violate a specific school rule or policy? You should never be punished for breaking a rule that didn't actually exist. A teacher can't decide after you've already done something to make a rule against it and punish you for what you've already done. He or she can forbid you to do whatever it is in the future, but must not punish you for doing it before the rule existed.

If there already was such a rule, the next question to ask is: Was it generally known? If the answer is "no," the school may have no right to punish you at all. You should not be punished for violating a rule you had no way to know about. A word of caution: The question is not whether or not you actually *knew* about the rule. It's whether or not you *should have known*. If the rule was published to the student body, you are bound by it whether or not you were aware of it yourself.

A rule can be published in many ways. Most schools have a handbook for students and parents that spells out school rules and policies. But rules can be published in other ways as well. They can be posted on school bulletin boards or printed in the school paper. "Published" doesn't necessarily mean "written" either. A rule might be published by being announced over the school loudspeaker system or at a school assembly.

The next important question to ask is: Is the punishment to be inflicted on you the one the rule calls for? School officials cannot threaten you with one penalty and then hit you with another more serious one.

Even if the punishment *is* called for in the rule, is it a reasonable punishment for the offense? There is an old saying that "the punishment must fit the crime." A school cannot expel someone for being late to class a few times, or flunk them for lighting a cigarette on school grounds.

Suspension and Expulsion

The most serious punishment your school can inflict is to deny you your right to an education. It can do this either temporarily, by suspending you; or permanently, by expelling you. Before school officials can impose such drastic punishment they need to give you a full and fair hearing.

This was decided in a landmark 1975 Supreme

Court decision known as *Goss* v. *Lopez*. It involved the cases of many students, all of whom had been suspended from schools in Columbus, Ohio, for various reasons. One of them, Dwight Lopez, had been suspended for ten days along with more than seventy other students after a destructive melee in the cafeteria at Central High. Dwight claimed that he was innocent, and there was no evidence that he had taken any part in the melee. And yet the school included him in the mass suspension, without giving him a chance for a hearing.

The Supreme Court ruled that Dwight and the other students had been denied due process. The right to an education is an important right. And the denial of that right is a serious matter. "[T]he total exclusion from the educational process for more than a trivial period . . . is a serious event," the Court declared.[3] Before a school can suspend someone for that long, the Court decided, it has to give them a fair chance to defend themselves.

Thanks to *Goss* v. *Lopez*, you are legally entitled to a full hearing before your school can expel you, or even suspend you for "more than a trivial period." This right involves several other rights. You must be given advance notice of the time and place of the hearing and of any evidence the school claims to have against you. You have the right to have a lawyer with you if you want to and to cross-examine any witnesses the school presents against you. You also have the right to testify yourself—or not to testify—as you wish. The decision of the hearing officer must be given to you in writing. In some states, you also have the right to appeal a decision that goes against you to some higher authority.[4]

Your Right to Obey Your Conscience

No teacher can make you do anything that violates your conscience. If you are asked to do something that conflicts with your religion, you have the right to refuse to do it. As long ago as 1921 a court ruled that children whose religion forbid them to dance did not have to take part in dancing exercises in gym class.[5]

The students in that case had to reveal their religious beliefs to be excused. But you don't need to belong to a religion to have serious moral objections to doing certain things. Some courts have recognized this fact while others have not.[6]

Teachers cannot force you to do things that conflict with certain deep political beliefs either. You cannot even be required to salute the flag or to recite the Pledge of Allegiance, if doing so goes against your conscience.[7]

In roughly half the states, you have the right to be excused from classes you (or your parents) object to on religious or other moral grounds.[8] If you are excused, however, you will probably have to take another class to make up for the one you miss.

Your Right to Read

You have a right to read anything you like. No teacher or

school official has the right to forbid you to read anything. Teachers do, however, have the right to decide what reading they will accept as fulfilling class reading requirements. And school libraries do have the right to decide what they will have on their shelves.

In other words, school officials cannot keep you from reading what you want to read, but they don't have to provide it to you. And they don't have to give you credit for reading it either.

On the other hand, teachers do have the right to give out reading assignments. In this sense they *can* tell you what to read. Occasionally such an order might conflict with a student's religion or conscience. An Islamic student, for example, might object to reading a book that makes fun of Mohammed. A Roman Catholic might object to reading a book that was on the Roman Catholic Church's Index of Forbidden Books. In such a case, you should ask that the teacher allow you to read something else instead. Most teachers will be more than willing to do so. In many states they are legally required to do so.[9]

Your Right to Privacy in Class

Among the rights you carry with you into the classroom is a right we've already talked about in Chapter Three— the right to privacy.

The freedom to speak also implies the freedom *not* to speak. This implies the right to keep silent about personal matters. In general, you don't have to reveal

You have the right to read anything you like. No teacher or school official has the right to forbid you to read anything.

things about yourself and your family you would rather keep to yourself. This can become an important issue in the classroom when teachers encourage you to reveal intimate information about yourself or to describe political, moral, and social beliefs.

Teachers do this in many ways, both directly and indirectly. An English teacher might ask you to write an essay dealing with a conflict between you and your parents. A social studies teacher might ask you to compare your family's financial situation with those of other students. A history teacher might encourage a debate between students on the wisdom of some government policy.

Teachers don't ask you to reveal these things out of idle curiosity or a wish to pry. Often they don't even realize that they are asking you to share private thoughts and information. They are merely encouraging you to talk or write. At other times they have good reasons for asking about these matters—or what seem like good reasons to them. Many teachers are sincerely concerned about your well-being and personal development. They may want you to discuss certain personal matters as a way of helping you to grow and mature.

Whether deliberately or not, teachers rarely have a right to make you reveal potentially controversial or embarrassing information about yourself. (And, in fact, most teachers would not want to do that.) They also do not have the right to know: (1) the details of any emotional problems you might be going through; (2) whether or not you take part in sexual activity; (3) how you get along with your family; (4) what church you go to—if any; (5) what political organizations you belong to; (6) what kind of medical treatment you're getting—unless your medical condition interferes with your ability to function in class; (7) any other purely personal information about yourself. You are perfectly free to share any of this information with your teachers but they have no right to demand that you do so.

On the other hand, teachers and other school officials do have a right to know some things about you. They need to know your age and sex, for example, in order to place you in the right grade and classes. They also have the right to require that you do reasonable assignments. These may well include papers or class discussions in which you are asked to describe certain thoughts and feelings.

Just what teachers should and should not be able to ask you about is a subject of much debate. One thing is clear, however; teachers in a public school have no right to ask about your religious beliefs. No public school teacher or other official has the right to know what religion you belong to, or if you belong to any religion at all. Even asking you to write a paper describing a family visit to church may be a violation of your rights.

Beyond religion, though, the lines over what is and what is not an invasion of student privacy are unclear.

Some parents object to students being asked anything that might reveal their opinions on any controversial subjects. Educators, however, tend to agree with Professor Edward Jenkinson of Indiana University, who insists that "asking questions to probe what students understand and to encourage them to think is basic to good teaching."[10] Other teachers agree that encouraging debate on controversial issues is an important part of educating good citizens.

Many students resent being asked to discuss family affairs or personal tragedies in class. They feel, as one educator has said, that they are being asked to "barter" their personal lives "for grades."[11] You should never have to do this.

The Hatch Amendment

Defenders of privacy rights in the classroom point to the Hatch Amendment to the General Education Provisions Act of 1978. The amendment protects students from being forced to take part in "any applicable program" designed to reveal information concerning—among other things—political affiliations, emotional problems, sexual behavior, income, or family relationships.[12] Some educators argue that the Hatch Amendment is really limited to certain federal programs, and shouldn't be applied to ordinary teachers operating in local classrooms. Nonetheless the amendment provides a good guide to those areas students have the clearest right to keep private.

Senator Orrin Hatch, the author of the Hatch Amendment, which helps students preserve their privacy from the prying of teachers and school officials.

Ultimately you have to be the one who sets the limits on your own privacy. If a particular question or assignment makes you uncomfortable, explain to the teacher that you don't want to talk about it. Ask for a substitute assignment. Most of the time the teacher will be sympathetic. If not, feel free to refuse to continue the discussion or assignment. Your privacy belongs to you. You are the one to decide what you will keep to yourself and what you will share.

7

Defending Your Rights

In this chapter we will outline some steps you can take to establish, protect, and defend your rights in school. These measures are very general. They may not all apply in all cases. But they will give you some idea of what you can do when you believe that your rights are being violated.

In the School

In most cases of conflict the best place to start is where the trouble is. If your problem is with a teacher, talk it over with him or her. Explain exactly what you believe your rights are and how you think they are being violated. Be polite and respectful, and present your arguments calmly and quietly. You will not convince a teacher of anything by angering him or her.

You may be able to convince the teacher to recognize

your rights. If not, you don't have to give up. There are higher authorities to whom you can appeal. The National Committee for Citizens in Education recommends that you follow your school system's "chain of command."[1]

In most cases the first avenue of appeal after the teacher is your school principal. If you can't convince the principal, your next step is to go to the local superintendent of schools. This person works for the school board and oversees all the teachers and administrators in the district. If the superintendent rules against you, you can appeal to the school board—which has authority over all the schools in your district. The school board can overrule virtually any decision made by a particular school administration. And even if the school board rejects you, you can appeal to the State Board of Education, which has the right to set many policies for all the schools in your state.

Remember that if you are ever threatened with suspension or worse, you have the right to demand a hearing before a neutral person or board. Even if some lesser punishment is involved, you can still *ask* for a hearing. In such cases, the school may not have to give you one, but many will.

Gathering Support

If there is an issue of school policy at stake, it probably affects many students besides yourself. Look for help among the student body or even among faculty members.

There are many things you can do to arouse support for your position. Talk to teachers whom you think might be sympathetic. If it is a freedom of press issue, for instance, talk to your journalism or English teacher. If your school has a student council, talk to your representative. Write a letter to the school paper or circulate a petition. Broad support within the school could help you persuade the authorities to change their position.

Parents

Perhaps the single most important place you can go for help is your own home. Having your mother or father on your side can mean a lot.

Unfortunately school officials often take complaints made by parents more seriously than the same complaints made by students. Hence parents can "carry more weight." What's more, parents are in a better position to threaten legal or other action if the school refuses to respect their child's rights.

Having your parents behind you can help in other more personal ways as well. As Brian Wilkinson wrote of his father's help during his and his brother's long battle with their school over the length of their hair: "Our family has grown closer. . . . We understand each other better and are more aware of our values."[2]

Defending your rights doesn't always produce this

kind of family unity, however. Your parents might not be as sympathetic as Dub Wilkinson. They might be embarrassed and upset with you for "making trouble." Instead of drawing you closer, your effort to defend your rights could push you apart. But this is probably more likely to happen if you act without telling them about what you're doing, than if you appeal to them for help.

You might be surprised how sympathetic they are. In Jasper, Alabama, a whole group of parents got together with their sons and daughters to fight an unreasonable dress code at Walker High School.[3]

Checking Your State's Law

As early as possible you should find out if your state has any laws that can help you protect your rights. Many states have laws that govern the rules school boards can set. If your school's policy seems unfair to you, it might conflict with these laws. Check your local library. If you can't find what you need there, your school board should know about state laws that apply. Even if the board disagrees with you, it should be willing to provide you copies of these laws. If your local board can't—or won't—your State Board of Education should. Your state representative might be willing to help you deal with these authorities. Checking your state's laws can be vital. Because if your school's rules violate state law, they cannot be enforced against you.[4]

Laws are written in complicated legalese, which

makes them difficult to understand. If you haven't already gotten legal help of some kind, you may need it when it comes to interpreting them.

Getting Legal Help

The ACLU recommends that you get legal help whenever you feel that your rights are being abused.[5] Lawyers' fees can be expensive, however. If you and your family can't afford to pay a lawyer (or if your parents are unsympathetic), you might be able to find an agency willing to help you for free.

The ACLU, itself, takes on cases in which it believes fundamental constitutional rights are being violated. Also many communities have legal aid offices whose lawyers represent people who can't afford to pay for legal services. These offices tend to be swamped with cases, however.

Check to see if there's a citizen's group in your community concerned with the particular right being violated. If your problem involves the right to practice your religion, you might appeal to a church, synagogue, or other religious body for help. If racial discrimination is involved, a local civil rights group might be willing to take up your cause. If it's a matter of sex discrimination, a feminist organization might be able to help. Some communities even have student advocacy groups that will help with virtually any kind of student's rights problem.

If you don't know where else to turn, call the Youth

Law Center in Des Moines, Iowa. The center may be able to advise you or to direct you to someone who can. Its address and telephone number, as well as those of several other organizations interested in the rights of young people, are listed at the end of this book.

Going to Court

If all else fails, you and your lawyer may decide that the only option left is to go to court. For young people, as for adults, courts are often the final defendants of their rights. Courts have enormous power in our society. Provided they agree that the law is on your side, they can overrule virtually ever other level of authority on your behalf. In 1992, a court in Florida even granted a Florida boy a kind of "divorce" from his own mother, on the grounds that she had not been a fit parent to him for many years.

The decision to go to court should never be taken lightly. It should usually be considered only as a last resort. In some cases, however, you may find—like many of the young people talked about in this book—that it is the only way you have to protect your rights.

Once the decision to go to court is made, you will be faced with a variety of other difficult decisions. One of the first will be what kind of lawsuit to file. In most cases, you will be suing primarily to prevent the school from abusing your rights. If some action of school officials has caused you serious harm, however, you may also be able to sue for money damages.

In order to win this kind of case, you need to do more than show that school officials violated your rights. You need to show that they did it deliberately—knowing very well that what they were doing was wrong.[6]

This is a hard thing to prove, and so it is rare for a student to actually win money from school officials. But the threat of this kind of suit can be a powerful encouragement to school officials to recognize your rights.

Another important decision you will need to make is whether to sue in federal court or state court. As we have seen, many states have laws that grant students even more rights than they have under the U.S. Constitution alone. But some state courts are actually less sympathetic to students than the federal district court in that region of the country. Your lawyer will advise you on these, and the many other, important decisions you will have to make.

How Much Are Your Rights Worth?

In the Declaration of Independence, Thomas Jefferson described our fundamental rights as "inalienable"—which means that they cannot be taken away. Even today we talk about "having" certain rights, as though they were permanent possessions.

In a sense our rights really *are* inalienable. They are ours by birth, and we are entitled to them until the day we die. But this way of talking about our rights can mislead us into taking them for granted. Because, in another sense, our rights are not permanent at all. They can be—and often are—denied.

Instead of saying that we "have" rights, it might be better to say that we *hold* them. Every right we have today, someone had to fight for and pass on to us. We will only continue to have them so long as we value them and defend them.

There may come a time when your rights are

threatened, either in school or somewhere else. When that happens, you will have to decide whether or not to fight for them. And you will have to decide how hard to fight.

It is important to be realistic in making these decisions. The battle to defend your rights can be long, hard, and expensive. There are always risks involved. At the very least you will annoy some school officials. You might have negative comments about you put in your school records. (If so, remember that you have the right to put your defense in there too.) At worst you may even be expelled. And, when it's all over, you might end up losing the battle: Your rights might still be denied.

It is up to you to decide how much your rights are worth to you, and how much you are willing to risk to defend them. While you are deciding, however, remember that your rights don't just belong to you. They belong to other people too.

You have the rights you have today because brave and determined young people—such as the Tinkers, Matthew Roberts, Christopher Eckhardt, the Wilkinsons, Lisa Rowe, Colin Murphy, Cathy Kuhlmeier, Dwight Lopez, and many others—fought for them and passed them on to you. It is up to you to decide whether you will pass them on to others.

Glossary

This glossary is not a dictionary. And it is not designed to give all the possible meanings of the words listed. Instead it is intended to help readers understand the way the following terms are used in this book.

absolute—Without exception.

appeals court, or court of appeal—A court that reviews the decisions of a lower court to decide whether they were legally correct. There are both state and federal appeals courts.

Buckley Amendment—A law that gives students and parents certain rights, including the right to examine the student's school records.

constitutional—According to the U.S. Constitution; anything that is required by a state or federal constitution; anything that is *not* forbidden by a constitution.

Constitution of the United States—The fundamental law of the nation; no federal or state law is valid if it contradicts the U.S. Constitution.

disrupt—To disturb or destroy normal order and discipline.

due process—The government's obligation to provide safeguards and follow legal procedures before punishing or penalizing someone.

duty—An obligation to do something.

exclusionary rule—The legal principle that keeps evidence discovered by unconstitutional means from being used in a trial.

expulsion—A form of punishment in which a student is permanently forbidden to return to school.

federal courts—Courts that decide cases according to federal laws and the U.S. Constitution (*See also* state courts.)

freedom—The right or ability to do something without interference.

freedom of religion—A right guaranteed by the First Amendment to the U.S. Constitution.

freedom of speech—A right guaranteed by the First Amendment to the U.S. Constitution.

freedom of the press—A right guaranteed by the First Amendment to the U.S. Constitution.

Goss* v. *Lopez—The case in which the U.S. Supreme Court ruled that a student cannot be suspended from school without due process.

Hatch Amendment—A law that protects students from being forced to reveal personal information about themselves to school authorities.

Hazelwood School District* v. *Kuhlmeier—The case in which the U.S. Supreme Court ruled that student journalists are not always fully protected by the First Amendment.

human rights—Rights based on moral and philosophical beliefs, instead of on specific laws; rights that belong to all people, wherever they live.

intrusive—Forced on someone without permission.

legal—Any action or policy that is either required or not forbidden by law.

legal right—A right that is established and protected by law.

libel—Untrue writing that damages a person's reputation.

minor—A person under the legal age of adulthood.

New Jersey v. *T.L.O.*—The landmark case in which the U.S. Supreme Court ruled that school officials could search students without probable cause.

obscenity—Speech or writing that is so morally offensive that courts rule it is not protected by the First Amendment.

parochial school—A private school run by a religious body.

private school—A school that is not part of a public school system and that does not depend on taxes for support. Students in private schools may not have all the same rights and protections as those in public schools.

privacy—The "right to be left alone."

probable cause—A good reason to believe that a crime

has been committed and/or that a specific person has committed it.

public forum—A publication that is open, "by policy and practice," to the free expression of any point of view.

published—Made known; in most cases, school rules must be published to the student body before they can be enforced.

reasonable—Done with good reason; sensible; Courts tend to uphold any school rule or policy they consider to be reasonable.

religious school—A private school that teaches the principles of a particular religion.

right—A just claim to some type of freedom, power, or privilege.

state courts—Courts that decide cases according to the constitution and the laws of a particular state. (*See also* federal courts.)

strip search—A search in which a person is made to remove some or all of his or her clothes.

sue—To bring a legal proceeding against a person or organization.

suspension—A form of punishment in which a student is forbidden to attend school, or regular classes within school, for a limited period of time.

Tinker* v. *Des Moines—The landmark case in which the U.S. Supreme Court declared that students and teachers do not "shed their constitutional rights to freedom of speech or expression at the schoolhouse gate."

trial—A legal proceeding in which evidence and arguments are presented on each side, and a decision is reached.

United States Supreme Court—The highest court in the United States. It decides, among other things, whether laws and lower court decisions are permitted by the U.S. Constitution.

unreasonable search, unreasonable seizure—Any search by authorities of a person or property, that is done without sufficient reason; the seizure of private property without sufficient reason. Unreasonable searches and seizures are forbidden by the U.S. Constitution.

waive—To give up a right.

warrant—An order by a court, directing police or other authorities to take a particular action.

Chapter Notes

Chapter 1

1. *West Virginia State Board of Education v. Barnette,* 319 U.S. 625 (1943).

2. *Tinker et. al v. Des Moines Independent Community School District,* 303 U.S. 503 (1969).

3. Ross R. and Patricia J. Olney, *Up Against the Law* (New York: Lodestar, 1985), p. 11.

4. Ibid., p. 11.

5. Sam and Beryl Epstein, *Kids in Court* (New York: Four Winds Press, 1982), p. 45.

6. "Free to Speak Out—With Limits," *Senior Scholastic,* March 14, 1969, p. 14.

7. *Tinker.*

8. Ibid.

Chapter 2

1. David Schimmel and Louis Fischer, *Parents, Schools, and the Law* (Columbia, Md.: National Committee for Citizens in Education, 1987), pp. 19–23.

Chapter 3

1. *The U.N. Declaration of Human Rights,* Article 12. Available from the U.N.

2. Paul Weckstein, *School Discipline and Student Rights: An Advocate's Manual,* (Cambridge, Mass.: Center for Law and Education, 1982), p. 165.

3. Kay E. Vandergrift, "Privacy, Schooling, and Minors," *School Library Journal,* January 1991, p. 26.

4. Nancy Schuessler, "A Question of Rights," *Seventeen,* May, 1989, p. 192.

5. *New Jersey v. T.L.O.,* 105 Sup. Ct. 733, 741 (1985).

6. Lowell C. Rose, "'Reasonableness'—The High Court's New Standard for Cases Involving Student Rights," *Phi Delta Kappan,* April 1988, p. 590.

7. *New Jersey v. T.L.O.*

8. Schuessler, p. 207.

9. *Doe v. Renfrow,* 1012 (N.D. Ind. 1979); *aff'd,* 631 F.2d 977 (6th Cir. 1984).

10. Janet R. Price, Alan H. Levine, and Eve Cary, *The Rights of Students: The Basic ACLU Guide to a Student's Rights,* Third Edition (Carbondale and Edwardsville, Ill.: Southern Illinois University Press, 1988), p. 88.

11. Ibid., p. 85; and Olney, p. 13.

12. Price, p. 87.

13. Ibid., pp. 138–139.

14. Ibid., pp. 136–137.

15. David Schimmel and Louis Fischer, *Parents,*

Schools, and the Law (Columbia, Md.: National Committee for Citizens in Education, 1987), p. 1972.

16. Ibid., p. 171.

17. Price, p. 135.

18. Schimmel, p. 176.

19. Price, p. 138.

Chapter 4

1. Devery Quandt, interviewed by author.

2. "Chilling the Fashion Rage," *Time,* January 22, 1990, p. 27; and Paula A. Poda, "Voluntary Dress Code Part of New School Year for Some," *Milwaukee Sentinel,* August 26, 1991.

3. Brian Wilkinson tells his own story in "Growing Dissent: The Politics of Hair," *Seventeen,* May 1990, p. 98.

4. Tim Allis, "Arguing that Sloppy Duds Make Sloppy Minds, Schools Fight to Revive Stricter Dress Codes," *People,* Oct. 23, 1989, p. 75.

5. Ross R. and Patricia J. Olney, *Up Against the Law,* (New York: Lodestar, 1985), p. 9.

6. *Arnold v. Carpenter,* 459 F.2d 939 (7th Cir. 1972).

7. *Domico v. Rapides Parish School Board,* 675 F.2d 100 (5th Cir. 1982).

8. Janet R. Price, Alan H. Levine, and Eve Cary, *The Rights of Students: The Basic ACLU Guide to a Student's Rights,* Third Edition (Carbondale and Edwardsville, Ill.: Southern Illinois University Press, 1988), pp. 38–39.

9. "Suspended Students Gain Right to Wear Rebel Flag," *The New York Times,* April 23, 1991.

Chapter 5

1. Extensive quotes from the *Spectrum* stories appear in "'Reasonableness'—The High Court's New Standard for Cases Involving Student Rights," by Lowell C. Rose, *Phi Delta Kappan,* April 1988, p. 592 and beyond.

2. Perry A. Zirkel, "Narrowing the Spectrum of Student Expression," *Phi Delta Kappan,* April 1988, p. 609.

3. Debbie Fuchs, "Students Should Have Freedom of the Press, Too!" *Seventeen,* September 1987, p. 182.

4. This interpretation of the *Hazelwood* decision in this section is based largely on the *SPLC Hazelwood Packet,* a publication of the Student Press Law Center, Washington, D.C., 1992.

5. *Hazelwood School Dist. v. Kuhlmeier,* 108 S. Ct. (1988).

6. *Hazelwood Packet,* p. 2.

7. *Burch v. Barker,* 651 F. Supp. 1149 (W.D. Wash. 1987).

8. Perry A. Zirkel, "Bad Astra: The Other Side of the Spectrum," *Phi Delta Kappan,* May 1989, pp. 734–736.

9. "Student Gets 'Wacked'," *Student Press Law Center Report,* Spring 1992, p. 17.

10. "Principal Suspends Underground Editors for Refusing Review," *Student Press Law Center Report,* Winter 1991–1992, p. 14.

11. Mark Goodman, interviewed by the author, June 3, 1992.

12. Jacob Allerdice," First Amendment Rights and the Student Press," *Scholastic Update,* April 26, 1985, p. 9.

13. Goodman.

14. "Free Expression Gains Momentum," *Student Press Law Center Report,* Winter 1991–1992, p. 9.

15. "Legal Roulette," *Student Press Law Center Report,* Winter 1991–1992, p. 2.

Chapter 6

1. *Tinker et. al v. Des Moines Independent Community School District,* 303 U.S. 503 (1969).

2. Cory McClure, interviewed by the author, May 27, 1992.

3. *Goss v. Lopez,* 419 U.S. 565 (1975).

4. Janet R. Price, Alan H. Levine, and Eve Cary, *The Rights of Students: The Basic ACLU Guide to a Student's Rights,* Third Edition (Carbondale and Edwardsville, Ill.: Southern Illinois University Press, 1988), p. 71.

5. *Hardwich v. Board of Trustees,* 205 p. 49 (Cal. 1921).

6. David Schimmel and Louis Fischer, *Parent, Schools, and the Law* (Columbia, Md.: National Committee for Citizens in Education, 1987), p. 159.

7. Ann E. La Forge, "Children's Rights in School," *Good Housekeeping,* March 1991, p. 221.

8. *Parent Rights Card,* National Committee for Citizens in Education, Washington, D.C.

9. Ibid.

10. Edward Jenkinson, "Classroom Questions: Respect for Student Privacy Isn't Asking Too Much," *The American School Board Journal,* November 1989, p. 27.

11. Kay E. Vandergrift, "Privacy, Schooling, and Minors," *School Library Journal,* January 21, 1991, p. 28.

12. Jenkinson, p. 28.

Chapter 7

1. *How to Appeal,* a National Committee for Citizens in Education booklet, 1991 (un-numbered).

2. Brian Wilkinson, "Growing Dissent: The Politics of Hair," *Seventeen,* May 1990, p. 100.

3. Tim Allis, "Arguing that Sloppy Duds Make Sloppy Minds, Schools Fight to Revive Stricter Dress Codes," *People,* Oct. 23, 1989, p. 74.

4. Janet R. Price, Alan H. Levine, and Eve Cary, *The Rights of Students: The Basic ACLU Guide to a Student's Rights,* Third Edition (Carbondale and Edwardsville, Ill.: Southern Illinois University Press, 1988), p. 51.

5. Ibid., p. vii.

6. *Wood v. Strickland,* 420 U.S. 308 (1975).

Further Reading

Books

Epstein, Sam and Beryl. *Kids in Court.* New York: Four Winds Press, 1982.

Fox, Kenneth. *Everything You Need to Know About Your Legal Rights.* New York: Rosen Publishing Group, Inc., 1992.

Gottleib, Stephen. *A High School Student's Bill of Rights.* Bloomington, Ind.: ERIC Clearinghouse for Reading and Communications Skills and the ERIC Clearinghouse for Social Studies/Social Science Education, 1991.

Olney, Ross R. and Patricia J. *Up Against the Law: Your Legal Rights as a Minor.* New York: Lodestar, 1985.

Parker, Barbara and Stefanie Weiss. *Protecting the Freedom to Learn: A Citizen's Guide.* Washington, D.C.: People for the American Way, 1983.

Price, Janet R., Alan H. Levine, and Eve Cary. *The Rights of Students: The Basic ACLU Guide to a Student's Rights.* Third Edition. Carbondale and Edwardsville, Ill.: Southern Illinois University Press, 1988.

Schimmel, David, and Louis Fischer. *Parents, Schools, and the Law.* Columbia, Md.: National Committee for Citizens in Education, 1987.

Student Press Law Center. *Law of the Student Press.* Iowa City, Iowa: Quill and Scroll, School of Journalism and Mass Communications, University of Iowa.

Weckstein, Paul. *School Discipline and Student Rights: An Advocate's Manual.* Cambridge, Mass.: Center for Law and Education, 1982.

Magazines and Other Publications

The following publications concentrate on issues relating to young people's rights. Check *Reader's Guide to Periodicals* and other data sources at your library for listings of specific articles on related subjects appearing in other magazines.

Code of Student Rights and Responsibilities, National Education Association, West Haven, Conn.

How to Appeal, National Committee for Citizens in Education, Washington, D.C.

Parent Rights Card, National Committee for Citizens in Education, Washington, D.C.

Steps, National Coalition of Advocates for Students, Boston, Mass.

Student Press Law Center Report, Student Press Law Center, Washington, D.C.

For Further Information

The following organizations are able to provide more information on issues relating to the rights of young people.

American Civil Liberties
Union
633 Shatto Avenue
Los Angeles, CA 90005
(Also has several local offices across the country.)

National Center for
Youth Law
Suite 900
114 Sansome St.
San Francisco, CA 94104
(415) 543-3307

National Coalition
of Advocates for Students
100 Boylston Street
Suite 737
Boston, MA 02116
(617) 357-8507

National Committee for
Citizens in Education
10840 Little Patuxent Parkway
Suite 301
Columbia, MD 21044
(301) 596-5300

Student Press Law Center
1735 Eye Street, NW
Suite 504
Washington, D.C. 20006
(202) 466-5242

Youth Law Center
405 Shops Building
800 Walnut
Des Moines, IA 50309
(515) 244-1172

Index

111